Introduction to iPad and iPhone

I0004864

Exploring the Internet
The Safari App

© 2018 iTandCoffee

iOS 11 Edition

Special Sales and Supply Queries

For any information about buying this title in bulk quantities, or for supply of this title for educational or fund-raising purposes, contact iTandCoffee on **1300 885 420** or email **enquiry@itandcoffee.com.au**.

iTandCoffee classes and private appointments

For queries about classes and private appointments with iTandCoffee, call **1300 885 420** or email **enquiry@itandcoffee.com.au.**

iTandCoffee operates in and around Glen Iris, Victoria in Australia.

Introducing iTandCoffee ...

iTandCoffee is a Melbourne-based business that was founded in 2012, by IT professional Lynette Coulston.

Lynette and the staff at iTandCoffee have a passion for helping others - especially women of all ages - to enter and navigate the new, and often daunting, world of technology.

At iTandCoffee, **patience is our virtue.**

You'll find a welcoming smile, a relaxed cup of tea or coffee, and a genuine enthusiasm for helping you to gain the confidence to use and enjoy your technology.

With personalised appointments and small, friendly classes – either at our bright, comfortable, cafe-style shop in Glen Iris or at your place - we offer a brand of technology support and education that is so hard to find.

At iTandCoffee, you won't find young 'techies' who speak in a foreign language and move at a pace that leaves you floundering and 'bamboozled'!

Our focus is on helping you to use your technology in a way that enhances your personal and/or professional life – to feel more informed, organised, connected and entertained!

Call on iTandCoffee for help with all sorts of technology – Apple, Windows, iCloud, Evernote, Dropbox, all sorts of other Apps (including Microsoft Office products), getting you set up on the internet, setting up a printer, and so much more.

Here are just some of the topics covered in our regular classes at iTandCoffee:

- Introduction to the iPad and iPhone
- The next step on your iPad and iPhone
- Bring your Busy Life under Control using the iPad and iPhone
- Making the Best Use of your Personal Technology
- Getting to know your Mac
- Understanding and using iCloud
- An Organised Life with Evernote
- Taking and Managing photos on the iPhone and iPad
- Travel with your iPad, iPhone and other technology.
- Keeping kids safe on the iPad, iPhone and iPod Touch.
- Staying Safe Online

The iTandCoffee website (itandcoffee.com.au) offers a wide variety of resources for those brave enough to venture online to learn more: handy hints for iPad, iPhone, Mac and more; videos and slideshows of iTandCoffee classes; guides on a range of topics; a blog covering all sorts of topical events.

We also produce a regular Handy Hint newsletter full of information that is of interest to our clients and subscribers.

Hopefully, that gives you a bit of a picture of iTandCoffee and what we are about. Please don't hesitate to iTandCoffee on 1300 885 420 to discuss our services or to make a booking.

We hope you enjoy this guide and find its contents informative and useful. Please feel free to offer feedback at feedback@itandcoffee.com.au.

Regards,

Lynette Coulston (iTandCoffee Owner)

Exploring the Internet
The Safari App

TABLE OF CONTENTS

Exploring the Internet
The Safari App

TABLE OF CONTENTS

Exploring the Internet
The Safari App

TABLE OF CONTENTS

Before we start ...

What is Safari?

Safari is Apple's **web browser** – just like Microsoft's Internet Explorer and Edge, Google's Chrome and Firefox (just to name a few others).

The Safari App on your iPad, iPhone and iPod Touch provides a 'mobile' version of the Safari web browser that you may also use on your Mac computer (if you have one).

The Safari App allows you to explore the Internet on your device - to find specific web sites and web pages (e.g. www.itandcoffee.com.au), or to use a 'search phrase' to search for content that matches your phrase (e.g. "iPad Classes in Melbourne").

Web Browser vs Search Engine

So often I hear comments like "But I use Google – I don't want to use Safari" or questions like "What is the difference between Google and Safari?".

Google is a Search Engine, while Safari is a Web Browser.

If you are confused about the difference between a Web Browser and Search Engine, you are not alone.

A Search Engine is used within a Web Browser, to allow you to search the internet using 'search phrases' – for cases where you don't know the website that you wish to visit and need to look for sites that might meet your needs.

Visiting the website **www.google.com.au** in the Safari App will allow you to search using the Google Search Engine (the Australian version).

Visiting the web page **au.yahoo.com** in the Safari App will allow you to search using the Yahoo Search Engine (again, the Australian version).

In fact, the grey bar at the top of your Safari window (which says 'Search or enter website name') allows you to perform a search without having to first go to www.google.com.au or au.yahoo.com (or any other search engine's website).

We'll explain this further as we go.

Before we start ...

Safari's features

Safari features on your iPad and iPhone include:

- Ability to have multiple Web pages (as 'tabs' open at once;
- 'Bookmarking' of your frequently used or useful web pages, so that you can easily find them later;
- Easy access to your Favourite websites
- Syncing of your tabs, Bookmarks and Favourites via iCloud (so that you see them on all devices, including your computer);
- A great feature that allows you to save your frequently used pages as icons that look like apps on your Home Screen;
- Reader — a feature that allows viewing of articles without ads or clutter;
- Reading list — where you can collect articles to read later;
- Sharing of web content via email, messages or to social media sites;
- Printing and copying of pages.
- And more.

Getting Started with Safari

Before you can use Safari, you must first connect your iPad or iPhone to the Internet — either through a Wi-Fi connection, or through a mobile data/cellular connection with your Internet provider.

Tap the **Safari** icon on the **Home Screen**.

What you see first will depend on whether you have previously used Safari, and what web page you were visiting during that last visit.

You may see a screen something like that below, with a few 'squares' on it (perhaps a few less than mine shows below) — perhaps they will be 'squares' for Apple, Disney, ESPN, and a few others. We'll explain these shortly.

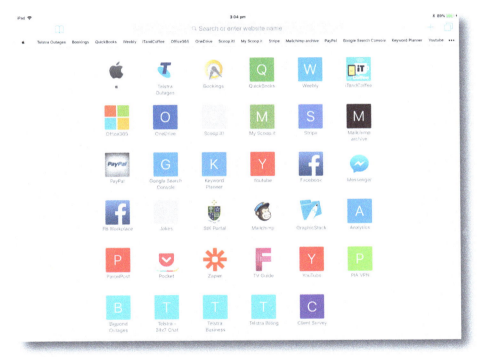

Alternatively, you may see the web page that you were looking at last time you opened Safari.

Whatever you see when you first open the Safari app, you can quickly get to when you want to go — so don't stress!

Getting Started with Safari

Looking at Safari on the iPad

Let's take a quick look at the key symbols and options available at the top of your iPad's Safari App.

Revisit recent pages -
< to go back;
> to return to the
page you just left.

See all your bookmarks,
reading list and
browsing history

Combined
Search and
Address field

Refresh the
web page

Add a new web
page tab

View all pages that
are currently open.
Swipe to delete
from here.

Choose from many
ways to share or
save – even print the
page.

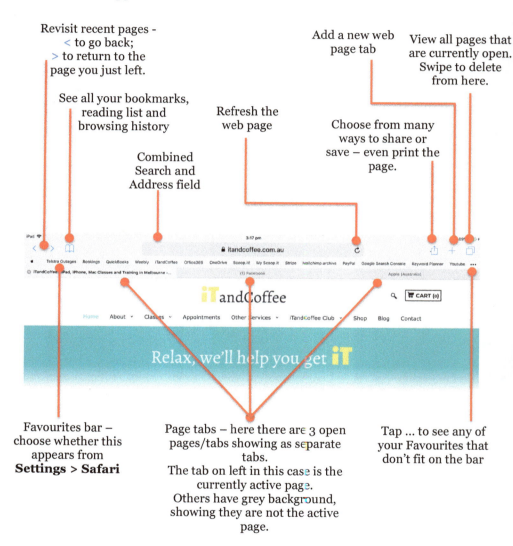

Favourites bar –
choose whether this
appears from
Settings > Safari

Page tabs – here there are 3 open
pages/tabs showing as separate
tabs.
The tab on left in this case is the
currently active page.
Others have grey background,
showing they are not the active
page.

Tap ... to see any of
your Favourites that
don't fit on the bar

Getting Started with Safari

Looking at Safari on the iPhone

The same options as shown on the previous page are also available on the iPhone. Because the iPhone is a smaller device, the symbols that appear at the top of the iPad instead appear at the bottom of the iPhone screen.

As on the iPad, the combined 'Search and Address' bar appears at the top of the screen.

If you have one of the newer 'Plus' iPhones, you may find that, when you turn your iPhone on its side, the options will move from the bottom to the top of your screen – making it look more like the iPad.

If you don't see the Safari search bar & options

You will notice when you are looking at a web page in Safari that, when you scroll down the page to view its details, the Search bar and other options will disappear. This is to give you more space to view the contents of the web page.

When you scroll back towards the top of the page, these options will re-appear.

A quick way to bring back the search bar and other options (without having to scroll back up the page) is to **tap near the time** (top middle of the screen, or top left on iPhone X). The Search bar and options will re-appear.

Searching for something

Getting started with your search

So, you are in Safari – what next?!

Well, it's time to start exploring the world-wide-web of interconnected pages – the Internet!

Tap in the Search bar at the top and type either

- your **search phrase** (for example, search for recipes with a particular set of ingredients – '*chicken capsicum mushroom recipe*') OR

- the **website address** (for example *www.itandcoffee.com.au*) to go directly to the website or webpage that you require.

But I can't see the keyboard!

Just touch on the Search field (or any other field that requires data to be entered) to make the keyboard appear if it is not currently visible.

Don't worry if you see a set of squares appear below the Search field on the iPad (as shown above).

On the iPhone, you will see that set of 'squares' take over your screen as soon as you tap the Search bar.

We'll talk about why you see these squares – and what they represent – shortly.

Searching for Something

But there's something already in the Search field!

The words from your previous search, or the web page that you have previously viewed, may already appear in your Search field.

Just touch on the  on the right-hand side of the Search field to clear out the previous information and type your new search.

If you notice that the previous search phrase (or address) is shaded in blue, just tap the **Backspace** key on the keyboard (or **Delete** key on the iPad Pro) to remove the highlighted text, so that you can type your new search. Alternatively, just type your new search phrase or address while the previous contents are highlighted in blue, and your typed text will be replaced the previous contents.

Cancelling your Search

If change your mind and decide that you don't want to search right now

- On the iPhone touch on the word on the word Cancel on the right of the search bar.

- On the iPad, you won't see a Cancel option. Simply touch anywhere to the left or right of the Search bar, or anywhere outside the white 'overlay' box that appears on when you touch the Search field and when you start typing.

Searching for Something

Completing your Search

If you want to go ahead with your search or your retrieval of a particular web page, tap **Go** on the Keyboard.

Looking for a specific web address

If you know the address of the web page that you require (for example, www.itandcoffee.com.au), just type it in to the Search field and touch **Go** on the keyboard - you will be taken straight to that page. It's a bit like when you know someone's phone number – you can call them directly by dialing the number, without having to look up the white or yellow pages!

Searching for Something

Make sure you type the address exactly as it should be – with no spaces, with the dots in the right places and with the correct ending (e.g. .com, .com.au, .net, .net.au, org.au, etc.). Leaving out any part of the ending could take you to a completely different website (or show there is no such website).

Searching when you don't know the web address

Sometimes, you don't know the address of the website you require, or you want to browse some options.

This is similar to the case where you need to look up the White pages for a phone number or peruse the Yellow Pages for a particular type of business or service.

The Internet provides so much more than phone numbers and business lookups.

Just type a 'search phrase' – a series of words describing what you are looking for. As you type in this search phrase, a list of search phrases similar to what you are typing will appear. The suggestions you see here depend on some Safari Settings (more on this soon).

In the below example, the search phrase is 'ipad classes in mel'. As this phrase is being entered, the list of suggestions appears.

Touch on a search phrase in the list if you see one that is applicable, or finish typing your phrase and select the **Go** key on the keyboard.

You will then see a list of results that match your phrase. We'll look at viewing and navigating your search results shortly.

Searching for Something

Searching for a word or phrase on the current web page

Occasionally, you may want to be able to find a particular word or set of words on the web page that you are currently viewing.

This is easy to do – just tap the option that appears at the bottom of the list of 'suggestions' that appear when you have typed your search word/phrase, under the sub-heading **On This Page** (see the image below left).

The number of matches for your search phrase may also be shown in this sub-heading.

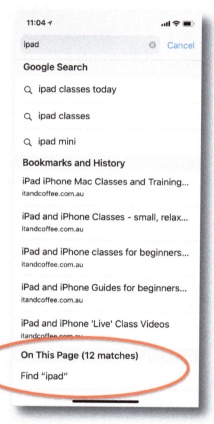 

When the item under this sub-heading is tapped, a grey bar appears at the bottom of the page (see image above right), with 'up' and 'down' arrow that allow you to find each occurrence of your search phrase on the page. In the example shown above, I have tapped the arrow key 4 times to see the fifth occurrence of the word iPad, which is highlighted in yellow.

Tap **Done** when you are finished viewing your page's search results.

Searching for Something

Paid results appear at the top

Sometimes, website owners pay money to have their websites appear prominently when certain 'keywords' are used.

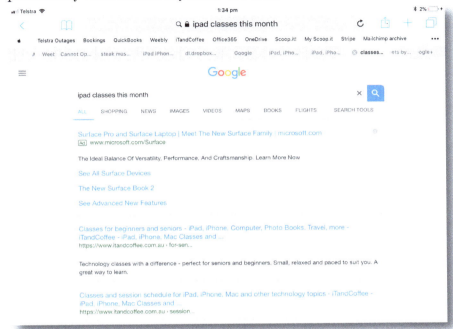

These results will be at the top or bottom of your list and will have an **Ad** tag on the left of the website address, identifying them as advertisements.

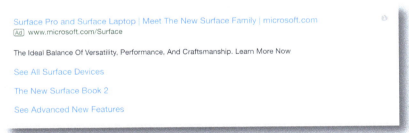

Just be aware that these ads are paid to appear based matches to just one or two of the words you have typed – so the page shown usually doesn't give you the best match. In the example above, you can see that the ad is for a Surface Pro - even though I was searching for iPad Classes!

I usually skip past these and look at the listings that don't have **Ad**.

Searching for Something

Tips for Searching the Web

Trying to find the website or web page that you are looking for can be tricky – working out the words to use to find what you need, and how to exclude results you don't want.

Here are some tips for ways to improve your search results and get just what you need.

1. Search for an exact phrase

If you are searching for an exact set of words (not just pages that includes the words anywhere on the page), put double quotation marks around the set of words.

2. Be more specific

If you want to find articles about managing your reading list in Safari on an iPhone running iOS 11, don't search for just **manage reading list**. Throw in all the words to more fully describe your search - i.e. **manage reading list safari iphone ios 11**. The more information you provide, the closer the search results will be to what you want.

3. Exclude a word

If your search is returning things completely unrelated to what you want (but that actually match your search), put a hyphen in front of any words that describe the thing you <u>don't</u> want.

An example is a search relating to a 'lightning cable' for charging your iPhone. You may get results about storms, thunderstorms, etc. So, add extra phrases like **-storm -thunderstorm -weather** to exclude any results that relate to the 'weather' form of lightning.

4. Use your own words

You can tap the microphone icon on left side of the spacebar on your keyboard (on the iPad) or at bottom right (on the iPhone), speak your search terms out loud, and then watch your device translate your words into typed text.

As soon as you finish talking, tap the small 'keyboard' at the bottom right and tap Go to perform your search. (We cover more on this in the iTandCoffee guide **Typing and Editing on the iPad and iPhone.**)

Searching for Something

Settings relating to Searching

In **Settings -> Safari**, there are several settings that relate to searching – settings that will determine what search engine is used by Safari, what suggestions are shown when you start typing in the Search bar, and more.

(In the below descriptions, any text in italics is taken directly from words that appear on the iPad/iPhone, describing that setting.)

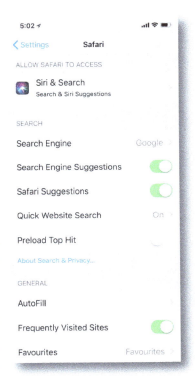

o **Search Engine:** Choose which search engine you prefer to use for your web browsing – options include Google, Yahoo, Bing or Duck Duck Go.

o **Search Engine Suggestions:** *"Safari will ask your selected search engine for suggestions based on what you've typed".* Turn this setting Off if you don't want to see such suggestions

o **Safari Suggestions:** As you type, Safari can show a list of suggestions for websites or search phrases, based on your past searches and other information. If you don't want these suggestions, turn off **Safari Suggestions**.

o **Quick Website Search:** This setting allows you to quickly search websites that have their own built-in search capability, without having to first go to that website and find the 'search' field. For this to work, you must visit the website once and do a search – and from that point on, you can use the Quick Website Search without having to go to the website first. For example, typing '*itandcoffee guides*' will find all iTandCoffee website pages that refer to 'guides'.

o **Pre-load Top Hit:** If this setting is 'on', *"As soon as Safari determines a 'Top Hit' based on your bookmarks and browsing history, Safari will begin loading the webpage in the background."* Turn this setting off to reduce how much data your Safari app uses by loading pages you don't necessarily want. Leave it on if you prefer 'responsiveness' over extra data usage.

Navigating on Safari

Browsing your Search results

If you have searched using a search phrase, peruse your list of results by dragging your finger up and down through the list.

When you see a result that looks of interest, touch on the **blue or purple** text – this is a **link** that takes you to the page that you have selected.

The link colour is **purple** (as shown in the second result above) if you have previously visited that web page. Otherwise, it is **blue**.

Returning to the previous page

When you have finished looking at that page, tap the < symbol at top left to return to the search results.

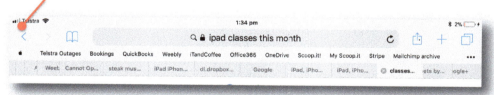

Then choose another blue or purple 'link' if you want to continue checking your search results / return to the previous page.

Navigating on Safari

Moving to the next page of results

When you reach the bottom of the page of search results, you will usually see a set of RELATED SEARCHES (giving you some similar search phrases that you might like to check).

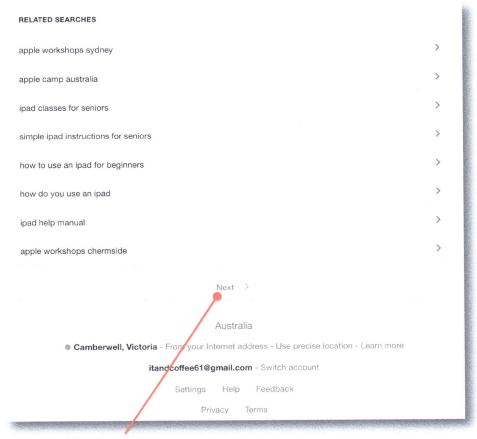

To continue looking at further search results for the phrase that you entered, selecting the **Next >** option towards the very bottom.

Navigating on Safari

Going back to previous page of results

When you are on the second and subsequent pages of your search results, the bottom of the page will show the 'page number' that you are currently looking at and provides < and > options to go to the 'next' or 'previous' search result pages.

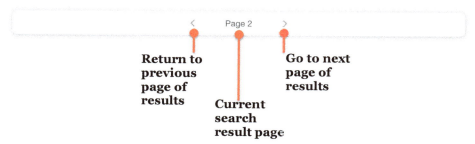

Alternatively, touch on the < at top left to return to the previous page of results.

Navigating around a web page

Scroll down the page by putting your finger on the screen and flicking or dragging upward. Return to the top of the page, put your finger on the screen and drag downwards.

> **Handy tip – return to the top of a web page quickly**
>
> To quickly return to the top of the web page when you have scrolled a long way down, tap near the very top of the screen (next to the time at top middle). This works in other apps as well.

'Zooming in' to enlarge what you are seeing

Double-tap the screen to enlarge the current web page's content – double-tap again to go back to previous size.

You can also use the 'pinch and spread' method with two fingers to enlarge or reduce the size of a web page on your screen – this allows you to view what's displayed at various sizes and gives more flexibility than the double-tap method.

Navigating on Safari

What if the page doesn't load

If for some reason a page doesn't display, or doesn't load properly, tap the **Reload** ↻ icon on the right end of the Search field – this will force Safari to try to access the site again.

If Safari is loading a web page and you change your mind about viewing the page, tap the Stop icon (the x), which appears on the right end of the Address field to stop loading the page.

Another way to move between web pages – the swipe!

An easy way to move between pages (instead of using the < and >) is to swipe across the screen (left-to-right and right-to-left) to perform the backwards and forwards functions that you would normally achieve with the < and > symbols.

Navigating on Safari

Make sure you start with your finger past the edge of the screen on either the right or left side. If you swipe your finger left or right from the middle of the screen, the 'Swipe' action won't work.

Following 'links' on web pages

On a web page, there may be lots of things called 'links' which, when tapped, take you to other pages on the current website - or perhaps take you to another website entirely.

Words on the page that represent 'links' are usually highlighted in blue, but could be another colour. They may or may not be underlined, depending on the website.

In the example on the right, the words classes, appointments, guides and videos are links to other web pages on the iTandCoffee website.

Links can also be attached to photos and other symbols that you see on the webpage

Patience is our virtue!

At iTandCoffee, you'll find a welcoming smile, a relaxed cup of tea or coffee, and a genuine enthusiasm for helping you to gain the confidence to use and enjoy your personal technology. Our technology *classes*, *appointments*, *guides* and *videos* are jargon-free and paced to suit you. If you can't come to our bright, friendly cafe-style shop in **Glen Iris Melbourne**, we can come to you*. If you live somewhere other than Melbourne, we have great online content to help you.

* Depends on your location.

To follow any link on a web page to another web page, just tap the link with your finger. The page you were viewing will be replaced by the page that is associated with the link.

Checking first where a link will take you

To view the destination web address of the link <u>before</u> you tap it, just **touch and hold the link**.

A menu appears that displays the destination address at the top.

You will see that this also gives you the options to choose the Open the page in the current **tab** (and replace the page you are currently viewing), Open in New Tab (in which case a new 'tab' is created with the link's page open on it), and a couple of other options. We'll talk about the concept of **tabs** shortly.

Navigating on Safari

Quickly return to a recently used web page

Touch and hold on the < or > symbols, to see a list of the websites you have just visited during your searching.

Touch on any page in the list to get to that page quickly.

This avoids you having to press the < or > multiple times to navigate back and forward – I use this frequently to return to my 'Search Results' after I have gone down several 'levels' of while perusing the results.

Multiple Web pages

Introducing 'tabs' for browsing multiple web pages

In Safari, you can have more than one web page open at a time.

On the iPad, the collection of open web pages is referred to, and represented as, **tabs** across the top. Here's an example of the Safari app on the iPad with lots of tabs currently open.

(On an iPhone, you don't actually see a list of open tabs/pages unless you access a particular option, which we'll look at shortly.)

Why would you use this?

The ability to have multiple pages open as 'tabs' is very handy when you have more than one page that you need to access and don't want to have to 'close' one to be able to access another.

In fact, if you tap on a link that is in an email or message (or some other place on your iPad or iPhone), Safari will automatically open a new page/tab and leave any previous tabs you had open.

So you might find yourself with multiple 'tabs' open without meaning this to happen.

Multiple web pages on the iPad

If you decide you would like to start a fresh tab to access a web page, simply choose the + symbol on the right-hand side to open another **tab**.

You will see a page appears straight away, showing square icons (that represent your **Favourite** websites) in the body of the screen (which we will cover soon).

Touch on one of these to go to that page, or type in your search phrase/address in the Search/Address field to find the required page for this new tab.

Multiple Web Pages

Moving between tabs on the iPad

Touch on a tab to bring that particular page to the fore/front. Touch on another tab to bring that other web page to the front. In the below example, to switch from the iTandCoffee page that is showing to the Facebook page's tab, I tap on the indicated tab.

Just imagine a stack of papers, where you keep switching which paper is on top of the pile! The 'active' tab has a lighter background than the 'inactive' tabs (which have a grey background).

Multiple web pages on the iPhone

Starting a new page, and moving between open Safari pages, is managed differently on the iPhone.

On the iPhone, tapping 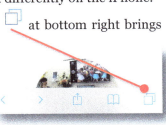 at bottom right brings up a the 'tabs' screen that looks something like that shown on the far right – a 'stack' of pages, representing all the web pages you currently have open.

Drag up and down to look through the pages that are shown, to see other pages that you currently have open.

Touch on the one you want to view it in full screen. Tap again to switch pages.

Touch + at bottom middle to open a new page.

We'll look shortly at another way you can quickly start a new page in Safari on the iPhone.

Multiple Web Pages

Keeping those open tabs under control

You can end up with numerous tabs open at once, especially when you have opened links that are included in emails and documents. Links on some web pages also cause a new tab to be added when you touch on them.

On the iPad, it is a good idea to regularly close tabs (i.e. web pages) that you are not using by touching on the little ⊗ that is on the left-hand side of the tab.

I must say that it can be hard to 'hit' this small ⊗. I prefer an alternative method (described next) of quickly closing web pages/tabs on my iPad.

An easier way of managing tabs

There is another way to 'close' open tabs that is a little easier than trying to hit that little ⊗.

On both the iPad and iPhone, your open tabs can be managed from the 'tabs' view.

On the iPad, a screen like that shown below will appear, showing the pages (tabs) you currently have open - as large thumbnails.

Multiple Web Pages

On the iPhone, you will see the screen that we described a bit earlier.

Pages/tabs that are no longer required can be quickly and easily 'closed' by **swiping the page to the left**.

Tap **Done** (top right on iPad, bottom right on iPhone) when finished your swiping.

Closing all open tabs/pages

Touching and holding on the 'tabs' symbol brings up a short list of options to help you manage your tabs and browsing (see below).

A really handy option in this menu is the Close all nn Tabs (where nn is the number of tabs/pages that you have open – 16 in my example below).

Quickly opening new tab on iPhone

Now that we have seen this menu of options - that can be accessed by touching and holding - you may notice another option available in this menu, the New Tab option.

Next time you need a new tab/page opened on your iPhone, tap and hold and choose New Tab.

Viewing two pages/tabs at once (iPad only)

This option is only available on certain iPads, when the iPad is in 'Landscape' mode. It is the Open Split View option available on your iPad when you touch and hold (see image above).

(iPad Mini's do not include this option. Other older iPads (depending on model) may not include the option.)

Multiple Web Pages

When you tap **Open Split View,** the screen will split in half, with two separate Safari 'sessions' appearing – allowing you to have numerous tabs/pages open in each half of the screen and then switch between tabs on either side of the screen.

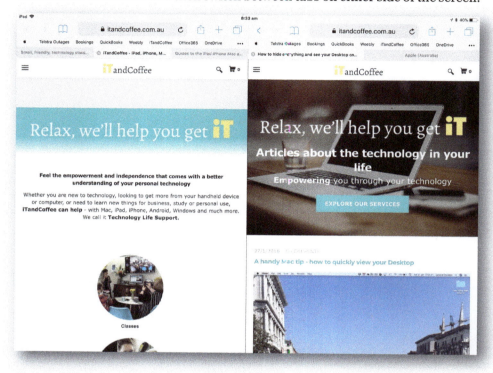

All the standard Safari options/symbols are available in the top bar on each side of the screen. It is like having two iPads sitting side-by-side, looking at the Safari app.

When the screen is in 'split' mode, touching and holding ⬜ again on either side of the split screen will show the **Merge All Tabs** option.

This will 'unsplit' the screen, and merge all the tabs that were open on either side of the screen into a single set of tabs when you are back in 'single page' mode.

Multiple Web Pages

Oops – I closed the wrong tab/page

If you ever accidentally close a page/tab that you now want to get back, this can be very easily achieved.

Just tap and hold the + symbol, which is visible on the main Safari screen on the iPad, and in the multi-page view of iPad and iPhone (accessed from the 'tab's view ☐).

You will see a list of recently closed pages - so just tap the one you want to re-open, and it will open as a new tab on your iPad or iPhone.

Safari and iCloud

If you have turned on **Safari** in iCloud, (in **Settings - > [your-name] -> iCloud**), you will see extra items listed at the bottom the list of web pages on your in the 'Tabs ☐ ' view.

This list shows the websites that you have open on another computer or on other i-Devices – any computer, iPad, or iPhone that is also linked to your iCloud, and has the **Safari** option turned on.

This option is very handy when you want to access a web page that you know that you were looking at on another device.

Multiple Web Pages

Settings relating to Tabs & Pages

In **Settings -> Safari**, there are several settings that relate to multiple web pages/tabs. We have covered some of them earlier in this section – here are the others that were not covered.

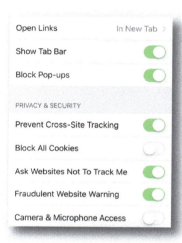

- o **Open Links (only on iPhone):** When you touch and hold on a link, you can choose to have one of two options appear:

    - o In New Tab – you will be taken to a new tab showing the link's page

    - o In Background – the link's page will open in a new tab, but you will stay on the current page.

- o **Open New Tabs in Background (only on iPad):** If this option is On, you will stay on the current page when you add a new tab – either by tapping a link or choosing +.

- o **Show Tab Bar:** Choose whether you want to see your tabs across the top of the Safari screen on your iPad (and 'Plus' iPhones in 'landscape' mode). If you turn this off, you will need to use the 'tabs' screen to move between open pages.

Sharing a Web Page

There is a variety of options for 'doing something with' a website that you have found.

You can send it to someone else via **Mail** or **Messages**, you can post it to **Facebook** and other social media sites, you can 'bookmark' it so you can find it again later, you can save it to your 'reading list', you can print it, and more.

All of these 'actions' can be found by touching on the 'Action' or 'Sharing' icon next to the Search field.

Just select the web page that you would like to do something with, and touch on the symbol.

Touch **Message** or **Mail** to send a **link to the web page** via Messages, email or some other messaging app, or to perhaps share it on Facebook.

We'll look at several of the other options in the 'Share' menu in the upcoming sections of this guide.

We'll also look soon at how you can, in some cases, send the content of the web page you are viewing, instead of just sending a link.

Your Favourite Web Pages on your Home Screen

This is a feature you will love! If you have a web page that you visit frequently, you can make it really easy to access it directly in future.

You can have the web page appear on your Home Screen, as an icon that looks like an App.

When you touch on the icon on your Home Screen, you will go directly to the page that you have chosen when you created the web page's icon.

Here are the steps for creating an icon for your favourite web pages:

1. Find the page that you want to see on your Home Screen. For example, type in www.itandcoffee.com.au to bring up the iTandCoffee website

2. Touch on the Share symbol.

3. Touch on the **Add to Home Screen** option in the second row. Your options may appear in a different order to those shown in the image on the far right, so drag from right to left to see more options.

4. You will then need to name the icon that you are creating – make sure you choose something brief, as it will be the name that is under the icon on the Home Screen. Tap on the name shown to change it.

   In the example shown here on the far right, I would change the long name that appears by default to just **iTandCoffee**, which gives the icon shown on right on my Home Screen.

5. Tap Add to complete the process of creating the icon on the Home Screen.

6. Your web page icon will appear in the next available position on the second or subsequent Home Screen.

Not all web pages will have a neat little icon like that shown for iTandCoffee. Sometimes, the icon will just show a mini version of what was showing on the web page you chose.

Printing a Web Page

Sometimes, you will find that you want to print a web page that you are viewing. If you have an Airprint compatible printer, this is very easy.

Once again, touch on the Share symbol ⬆ and then choose **Print** from the options shown in the second row.

Print

Once again, if you don't see the option in the second row, swipe right to left to see more options.

The print screen will appear, showing a preview of how the page will look when printed. Swipe through the pages to preview them.

Tap **Range** to choose which pages you wish to print – in the example shown below, there are 10 pages to print, but I can print just a few.

If the **Printer** field shows **Select Printer**, tap on this and tap on the name of your Wi Fi printer to choose it. If no printer is shown, then you may not be connected to your Wi Fi network, or your Airprint printer may not be connected to your Wi Fi network.

As mentioned earlier, the Wi Fi printer must have a feature called **Airprint** for the iPad or iPhone to be able to print to it.

Once you have selected your printer, you may see some further print options appear below the 'number of copies' field. Tap on any of these options to adjust your print settings.

Once you have done this, choose Print at top right to print your web page's contents to your Airprint printer.

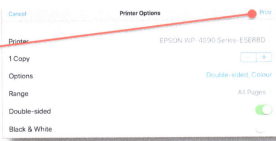

38

Saving a web page to your Reading List

When you visit a web page that you would like to read, but just don't have to time read it right now, you can use the **Reading List** feature to save it away for later reading – with or without an Internet connection!

Once again, tap the Action/Share button and then tap **Add to Reading List**.

Add to
Reading List

Or, if you see a link to a page on a Safari page (where 'links' are described earlier) and you decide you'd like to check out that web page later, touch and hold the link until a list of options appears.

Tap **Add to Reading List**.

We'll shortly look at how to access this Reading List – and how to choose which saved pages you want be able to access 'offline' (i.e. when you have no internet) – a bit later in this guide.

Bookmarking your Favourite Web Pages

Understanding Bookmarks and Favourites

'Bookmarking' means marking a particular website page as one that you want to find and return to easily – similar to placing a bookmark in a book.

Safari provides the capability to set **Bookmarks** on any number of web pages, and to categorise/group these Bookmarks.

There is a special category of Safari Bookmarks, known as your **Favourites.**

Any web page that you save as a **Favourites** bookmark will be shown on the screen you see when you open a new tab (with +) or tap on the 'search' field – the screen that shows a set of squares.

Below is the screen that appears on my iPad. You may not have quite as many squares as I do!

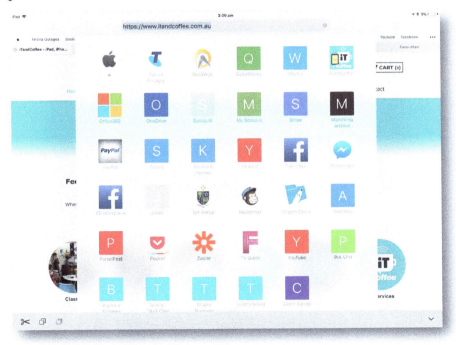

The idea of the Favourites screen is to provide quick and easy access to those 'bookmarked' web pages that you will access the most – your Favourites.

Bookmarking your favourite web pages

Let's look at how you can choose your own set of Favourite Bookmarks. We'll also look at how you can remove any 'squares' that you don't want to see any more – especially those provided to you by Apple as default Favourites.

Creating Favourites is quick and easy

Go to the page that you want to save – use the search techniques described earlier, or type in the web page's address.

Here's how to 'bookmark' that page as a Favourite.

1. Touch on the Share symbol.
2. Tap **Add to Favourites.**
3. Name your Favourite. It is best to make this name as short as possible. Touch the ⊗ to remove the default name and type in your own.
4. Then choose Save.

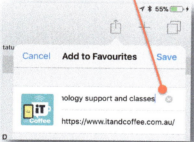

Your new 'favourite' will be added to your set of favourites, as the last one in the set of 'Favourites' squares.

We'll look shortly at how you can rearrange your Favourites so that the most frequently used appear first.

Creating a Bookmark

You may want to 'bookmark' a web page so that you can return to it at any point. However, you may not want it to be in your list of Favourites.

Here's how to bookmark a web page.

1. Go to the page that you want to save.
2. Touch on the Share symbol.
3. Touch on **Add Bookmark.**

Bookmarking your favourite web pages

4. As for saving Favourites, the first field shown is the name for the Bookmark – so enter a short name.

5. Now you need to choose where you want to put this Bookmark. If you are happy with the location that is shown in the LOCATION field, just tap Save.

6. If you want to store the Bookmark in a different Bookmark folder, tap the LOCATION value shown.   As list of you available Bookmark locations will be shown.

7. If you have never created any other 'bookmark folders' (which we will look at soon), you will only have the Bookmarks option in the list that appears.

8. Otherwise, you will see the list of folders that are available for storing your bookmarks.

9. Touch on the Bookmarks folder in which you would like to store the current bookmark (or just choose **Bookmarks** if you only see the **Bookmarks** folder).

10. Then choose Save to complete the Bookmark creation process.

We'll talk soon about how to create your own Bookmarks Folders

Managing all those 'squares' you see

The set of squares that you see when you add a new 'tab' or tap on the search field can be easily re-arranged and any squares that are no longer required can be removed.

You may also notice a section at the bottom of this screen showing some additional squares under the heading FREQUENTLY VISITED.

The FREQUENTLY VISITED set of squares represents the websites you have been found to visit the most on this device.

Let's look at how you can manage all these squares!

42

Bookmarking your favourite web pages

To move your squares around to change the order of your Favourites, just put your finger on a square until it 'pulses', then drag it to the required position. Easy!

To remove a square that represents a favourite that you no longer require, put your finger on the square until it pulses. Then let go, and you will see the **Delete** and **Edit** options.

Tap **Delete** to remove that favourite.

Tap **Edit** if you would like to change the name of that favourite; or to change the location of the favourite bookmark – for example, to remove the bookmark from Favourites, and store it in a different bookmark folder.

If you would prefer not to see the FREQUENTLY VISITED section at the bottom of this screen, visit **Settings -> Safari** and turn off **Frequently Visited Sites**.

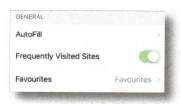

Make your Favourites visible all the time in Safari

On an iPad (but not an iPhone), you can also choose to show your set of **Favourite** web pages in a bar that appears below the search field – called the **Favourites Bar** - making it very easy to get to the pages you use frequently by just tapping on the name in the bar.

Bookmarking your favourite web pages

To turn on the display of this bar, go to

Settings > Safari > Show Favourites Bar.

If there are more favourites than can fit across the top of your iPad screen, then you will see ... at the right end of the Favourites Bar.

Tap on **...** to see the rest of your Favourites. Tap on the Favourite that you want to look at in Safari.

Sync your Bookmarks using iCloud

If you have more than one device – perhaps an iPad, iPhone and/or Mac, it can be so handy to sync your Safari Bookmarks with these other devices

This can be achieved really easily by ensuring that you turn 'on' the Safari option in your iCloud settings (as shown a bit earlier). This will allow you to see the same set of Bookmarks and Favourites on each device that is connected to your iCloud account.

Other Settings related to Bookmarks

We have covered several settings relating to bookmarks above, all found in **Settings->Safari**. There is one more that we didn't cover above:

o **Favourites:** Choose which Bookmarks folder to show in the Favourites screen and bar – by default, it is the Bookmarks folder called Favourites.

Viewing and Organising your Bookmarks

Viewing and selecting a saved Bookmark

You can end up with a long list of Bookmarks and you might like to organise these into Folders so that you can more easily find them in future. These Folders can help to categorise your Bookmarks.

The option for viewing and organising your Bookmarks is on the left of the Search field on the iPad, and on the bottom on the iPhone. Look for the symbol that looks like an open book.

Touch this symbol to view your saved Bookmarks, browsing history and your Reading List.

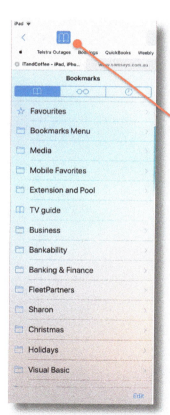

On the iPad, the Bookmark symbol at the top of the screen will then have a blue background and the Bookmarks sidebar will appear on the left of the screen. Tap the blue bookmark symbol again to hide the Bookmarks sidebar.

On the iPhone, the Bookmarks menu will take over the screen.

To see your Bookmarks, touch on the same 'book' symbol at the top of the list that you see – it is the leftmost symbol (as indicated here).

You will then see a list of your Bookmarks - mine are shown on the left, showing the folders into which I have organised my bookmarks.

On the right is what you would see in Bookmarks if you have not yet saved any bookmarks (to any place other than Favourites).

Viewing and Organising your Bookmarks

Creating a new Bookmark folder

When viewing your Bookmarks, select Edit at the bottom right

You will then see an 'edit mode' version of the screen with the New Folder option at the bottom.

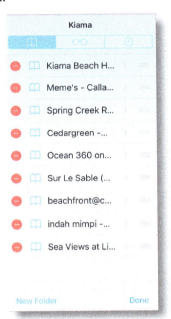

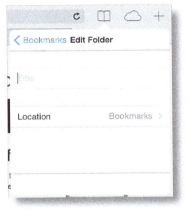

Create a **New Folder** by touching on this, then typing in a name for the folder in the **Title** field.

Then choose the place where you want the folder to reside (i.e. as a sub-folder of another folder that already exists, or under the main **Bookmarks** folder) by touching on **Location**.

When you have finished defining the bookmark folder name and location, press Done on the keyboard. When you have finished creating and managing your bookmarks, press Done at bottom right.

Viewing and Organising your Bookmarks

View contents of a Bookmarks Folders

When viewing the list of **Bookmarks**, there are two symbols that you might see –

- a bookmark symbol,
- and a folder symbol.

A folder is a collection of bookmarks (and, perhaps, includes other folders within that folder).

Tapping a Bookmark in this list will take you to that web page.

Tapping a Folder will show the contents of that folder.

For example, touching on the **Kiama** folder will give me the list of accommodation web pages that I looked at for the holiday destination **Kiama**.

To return to my 'top level' Bookmarks menu, I touch on < All towards the top of the **Kiama** folder.

Changing the location of a bookmark or folder

To change what folder a Bookmark or Bookmark Folder appears in...

1. Go to the Folder where the bookmark appears and select **Edit**.
2. Touch the applicable Bookmark from the list that appears.
3. Touch on the **Location** field
4. Choose the Bookmark's new folder location.

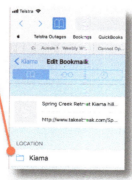

Viewing and Organising your Bookmarks

Deleting a bookmark

It's very easy to delete a Bookmark, or even an entire Bookmarks Folder.

1. Swipe any Bookmark or Folder you no longer require to the left – to see the **Delete** option.
2. Tap **Delete** to remove the bookmark/folder.
3. The Bookmark or folder will disappear from the list.

OR

4. Select **Edit** at bottom right
5. Just touch on the delete 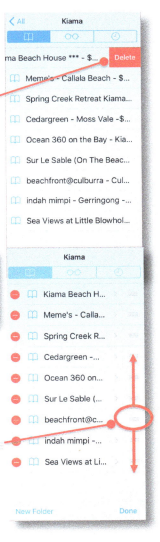 symbol on left of the folder or Bookmark that you want to delete.
6. Then tap **Delete** to confirm

   The bookmark or folder will disappear from the list.

Change the order of your bookmarks

To change the order of your bookmarks, you again need to get into the **Edit** mode.

Then, just hold your finger on the 'sort/re-arrange' symbol next to the item that you want to move and drag it up or down to the required position.

Easy!

Your Reading List

Earlier, we looked at how to save web pages to your Reading list so that you could get back to them later. Now let's look at viewing, using and managing this Reading List.

Reading a page on your Reading List:

Tap the Bookmarks icon 📖 on the main Safari screen to show the Bookmarks screen/sidebar

Tap on the 'glasses' symbol to view your **Reading List**. The background of this symbol will turn blue to show that is it active. 👓

Just tap on any web page in the list to read it now.

Keeping track of what you've read

You can choose whether to view just the unread items in your reading list, or whether you want to see all items in your list.

Choose '**Show All**' at the bottom to reveal your full list of read and unread web pages.

This option will then change to '**Show Unread**' – touch this phrase to change back to viewing only the 'Unread' web pages in your Reading list.

Removing items from the Reading List:

As we saw earlier for Bookmarks, just swipe the item from right to left and then choose the **Delete** option that appears on the right.

Reading offline

There may be times where you know that you won't have internet access but want to be able to access web pages that you have saved to your Reading List.

The **Save Offline** option (which appears when you swipe right to left on an item in your Reading List) allows for such pages to be saved to your device in full, so that internet access is not required to access them.

Your Reading List

A saved page can then be removed from your device by swiping from right to left again and selecting **Don't Save** (or **Delete** if you no longer need to keep it in your Reading List).

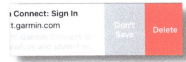

All Reading List pages offline

If you would rather have all pages you save to your Reading List made available offline, you can turn on the **Automatically Save Offline** settings in **Settings->Safari**.

Just make sure you don't end up using too much or your device's storage with these saved web pages.

Your Reading List in iCloud

If you have turned on **Safari** in your iCloud settings, you share your Reading List with all your other Apple devices – as long as they are also on the same iCloud and have the **Safari** option turned 'On'.

View your Safari browsing history

As you browse the Internet, Safari keeps a record of what web pages you have visited (unless your browsing is in Private Mode or using Duck Duck Go – more on these options in the next section).

This record can be handy when you want to visit a site that you viewed previously but have forgotten its address, or the search phrase you used to find it.

You can view the list of websites you have visited, by choosing one of the options option along the top of the Bookmarks screen/sidebar.

1. Tap the **Bookmarks** icon ▯ on the main Safari screen.
2. Tap the Clock icon on the right ⏱ – this is the **History** view.

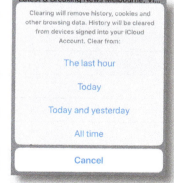

3. You will see a list of the sites you have visited, grouped according to the date that you visited.
4. Tap on any site in the list to revisit it.

To delete individual entries in the History list, swipe from right to left and choose **Delete**.

To clear your browsing history, tap **Clear** at the bottom right.

Choose from the options shown, to clear just some hours/days of history, or choose **All Time** to clear everything.

(If you have set up something called **Restrictions** on the iPad or iPhone, and have chosen to **Limit Adult Content** for Safari, then the **Clear** option won't be enabled. Instead it will be grey, indicating it is not available. Find out more about Restrictions in the iTandCoffee guide **Keeping Kids Safe on the iPad, iPhone and iPod Touch**.)

Discovering Reader

Uncluttered viewing of web pages

Safari has a great feature called **Reader**, which allows you to view certain web pages with just the text and images – and without the clutter of advertisements and other extras.

This is great for reading newspaper articles, recipes and more.

Not all web pages will provide you with this option – only those deemed to be 'articles'.

Look for pages that have a 'lines' symbol ☰ are on the left of the Search field.

When you tap the 'lines' symbol ☰, the article/page will come up stripped of all distractions and in easy-to-read text. The Reader symbol will then have a black background ▦ to show that Reader Mode is active.

In the images below, the left-hand image is the normal web page. The right-hand image is the **Reader** version - the dark background on the Reader symbol shows that it is on.

Discovering Reader

Using Reader whenever possible

With the arrival of iOS 11, the Reader feature has been updated to include the **Automatic Reader View** function.

Automatic Reader View allows the you to nominate that you want any page that is able to show Reader format to automatically show this format when you go to that page.

To activate **Automatic Reader View**, simply touch and hold on the Reader ☰ symbol to see a couple of options.

You can choose to activate the **Automatic Reader View** for individual compatible websites that you view, or for all compatible websites.

To turn off **Automatic Reader View**, touch and hold the Reader symbol again and choose to turn it off the all web pages, or just the current web page.

Handy Tip: Send full article in an email

Reader View can be very handy when you want to send the contents of an 'article' to someone via email.

Normally, sending a Safari web page will only send the link to the page – and the person who receives that link may not be able to access the page, especially if it is from a 'subscriber-only' website.

When the page is being viewed in **Reader** format, choosing to mail it to someone will result in an email that contains the content of the web page – words and images – and not just a link to the page.

Saving Website Images

Yes, you can save images that you see on a web page to your **Camera Roll** (or **All Photos)** in Photos.

In saying that, not all photos you see on a web page can be saved. You need to try out the below steps to determine if the image can be saved.

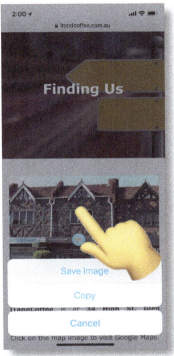

- Touch and hold the picture for a second or two.

- A menu appears giving you the option to Save Image, or to Copy it to the device's **clipboard**.

- Choose Save Image to save to your **Photos** app (to the Camera Roll/All Photos).

- If you Copy an image from a web page to the **clipboard**, you can then go somewhere else and **Paste** it – for example, add it to an email or a Note.

*The **clipboard** is an area in your device's memory where something that you have 'copied' or 'cut' is held, until you choose to 'Paste' it somewhere else, or until it replaced by another 'copy'.*

Private Browsing

If you are concerned to ensure that the information about your internet browsing is not stored or tracked, you can use something called **Private Mode**.

Private Mode allows you to browse the web without saving a record of browsing history, logins or searches. It protects you if someone gets hold of your iPhone/iPad – they can't see where you have been on the Internet.

However, you will lose the convenience of saved logins and things called cookies – this may mean that certain websites will not work as you expect.

Switching to Private Mode

To go into **Private** mode, tap the 'tabs' symbol ⬜ and tap the word **Private**.

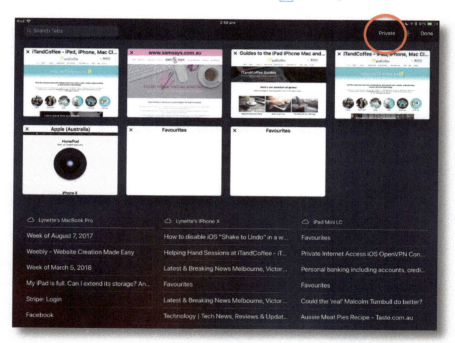

You'll notice that the word **Private** changes to have a white background, to indicate that you are now in **Private** mode. Any tabs that you have previously had open in **Private** mode will show.

Private Browsing

Tap on any of these tabs to return to that page or tap **Done** at top right to return to the main Safari screen.

How to spot Private Browsing mode

You will see that, when you return to the main Safari screen, the top of the screen shows a dark background instead of the normal white background. This is to distinguish **Private** mode.

Any tabs you open while in Private mode will not have any history or website data saved.

The set of tabs/pages that you open in Private mode are a separate set to those that you have open in non-Private mode. When you return to non-private mode, the pages/tabs that you had open will still be there.

You can switch between private and non-private modes – perhaps have a set of pages that you want to ensure are not tracked, and others than do not need to be so private.

Returning to non-Private Mode

To return to normal (not Private) mode, tap the **Tabs** symbol again and tap the word **Private** again.

The white background on the word Private will disappear, to show you are no longer in Private mode, and the pages/tabs you had open in this mode previously will re-appear.

A quick way to open a new page in Private Mode

A new 'Private' page can be opened quickly by touching and holding on the 'tabs' option and choosing the **New Private Tab** option.

You will switch to **Private Mode** and be able to choose the page that you wish to view in this mode.

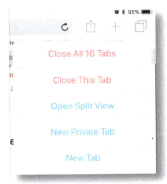

Private Browsing

You can choose Private Browsing always!

If it is important to you that your internet searches are not tracked, you can use a Search Engine called **Duck Duck Go** instead of **Google** as your default web browser.

This means the Duck Duck Go search engine will be used when you type a search phrase into the search bar of Safari.

Then, no advertisers or anyone else will be able to track your searches and movements in Safari.

This is achieved by visiting the **Search Engine** option in **Settings -> Safari**, and choosing **Duck Duck Go** as the default search

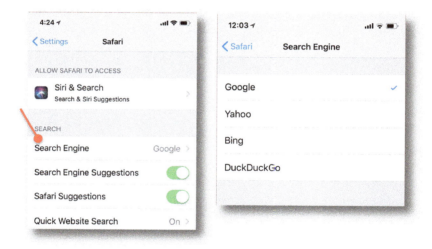

A Handy tip for Online Payments

If you are sick of typing in your credit card number for online payments, there is a handy feature of Safari that can help.

Safari provides the Scan Credit Card option whenever you are positioned on a credit card number field.

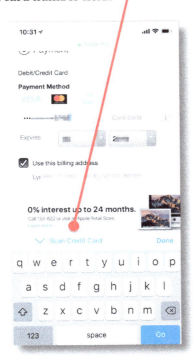 

Tap Scan Credit Card – and if you get a message asking if Safari can use the Camera, say yes.

Then, hold your device's camera above the credit card (as if you were taking a photo of the card), so that the card is (approximately) within the rectangle shown.

Your device will detect the card's numbers automatically – filling in the card number and expiry date fields quickly and easily.

You will then just need to add the card code (ccv/cvv) from the back of the card to complete the entry of your credit card details.

Autofill in Safari

The **Autofill** area of settings allows you to choose what information should be able to be filled in automatically for you based on information that has been stored on, and saved to, your device.

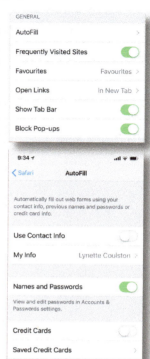

Some of that information is stored in your Contacts, in the Names and Passwords area of Settings, and in the Saved Credit Cards option under this Autofill setting.

Let's look at the **Autofill** options in **Settings->Safari**:

o **Use Contact Info** allows fields that are deemed to relate to names and addresses to offer the option fill the field from your list of contacts.

   I have chosen to turn off **Use Contact Info**, because I found that I could not properly access some fields in Safari when it was on.

o **My Info** allows you to define which Contacts card is your own, so that you can choose to auto-fill your own details in name and address fields of Safari.

o **Names and Passwords** allows Safari to auto-fill fields based on login/password details that have been saved to your device. The list of saved login/password details can be found in **Settings -> Names and Passwords**

o **Credit Cards** allows you to choose whether or not you would like Safari to automatically fill in credit card fields based on credit card information that have been saved/entered in **Saved Credit Cards**.

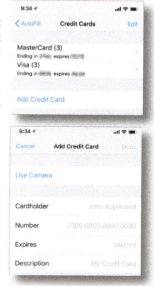

o **Saved Credit Cards** allows you to add (or remove) credit cards details that can be used by Safari (excluding ccv/cvv details).

   Choose **Add Credit Card** and enter details of a new Credit Card. Or **Use Camera** to scan in the card's details (as covered in the previous section).

   Choose **Edit** to edit or remove any credit cards already in the list.

More Safari Settings

There are various settings that you can adjust for your Safari app, many of which we have mentioned throughout this guide. In this section we will look at settings that have not been mentioned elsewhere in the guide.

Visit **Settings > Safari** to see the long list of settings for this app.

(Where you see text in double-quoted italics below, we have taken the description directly from descriptions that appear on the iPad and iPhone.)

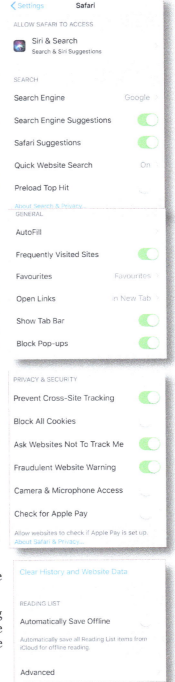

- **Siri & Search:** *"Allow information from 'Safari' to appear in Search, Look Up and Keyboard. Siri may learn from and make suggestions based on how you use this app."* Turn off this setting if you don't want to allow such use of Safari data.

- **Block Pop-ups:** When on, this setting blocks pop-up ads and other pop-up windows. Occasionally, you might find this also blocks something that needs to pop up and the web page won't work properly. If this occurs, you can temporarily turn this setting off, then turn it back on when you are finished with the page.

- **Prevent Cross-Site Tracking:** Set this to 'on', and Safari will attempt to stop websites from tracking your activities once you've left that website – for example, to stop those creepy adds that appear everywhere after you have looked at a product.

- **Block all Cookies:** A cookie is a piece of data that a website saves to your iPad or iPhone device so the website can remember you when you visit again. This also allows the webpage to be customized for you, based on information you may have previously provided.

  Important Note on blocking Cookies: Some pages may not work unless you accept cookies.

- **Camera & Microphone Access:** This setting determines whether Safari websites can use the built-in camera and microphone. If you are

More Safari Settings

concerned about privacy, you may want to leave this setting 'off' and just turn it on if you ever access a website that needs these facilities.

o **Check for Apple Pay:** Turn on this setting if you want to *"Allow websites to check if Apple Pay is set up"* so that you can pay online using Apple Pay

o **Fraudulent Website Warning**: Turn this on to receive a warning if you visit a website that is a suspected to be a fraudulent website, one that could attempt to steal your personal information - passwords, account information, or user names.

A fraudulent website (a phishing website) often pretends to be a real website – for example, a bank, financial institution, Facebook, PayPal, or email service provider. (We will cover fraudulent websites and browsing security shortly)

o **Clear History and Website Data**: Clear all of your device's browsing history, cookies and other browsing data from Safari. This history will be cleared from all devices signed into your iCloud account.

o **Advanced:** Under the Advanced option, you will find some further settings. We won't cover all of them here (as they are a bit 'techie'), but here are a couple worth knowing about:

 o **Enable or disable JavaScript**: JavaScript lets web programmers control elements of the page. For example, a page that uses JavaScript might display the current date and time or cause a linked page to appear in a new pop-up page.

 o **Website Data**: You can see what sites have stored data on your device (and how much), and can clear data relating to specific websites. You will see the option to **Remove All Website Data**. Alternatively, swipe from right to left across any of the listed websites and choose the **Delete** option to delete that particular website's stored data.

Staying Safe Online

The whole area of online safety really is something that all Safari and email users need to have in front of mind while browsing the internet and while interacting with emails, texts and other forms of online communication. This section is not intended to provide comprehensive information about this topic. Rather, it just reflects some things to consider in relation to your online safety.

Secure vs. Unsecure websites – http vs. https

Before providing any login details, private or financial information when using Safari, make sure that the website you are using has a 'lock' on the left.

Also check that the website address (known as its URL) has **https://** in front of it. Tap on the search bar to check the full address details of the page you are viewing.

This is essential if you are ever providing any personal or financial information, as a site that is just a http:// site is not secure - your information could be easily stolen.

(Warning!! Some scammers' websites can look like they are https but are not – you must still be careful to ensure you trust the site before providing any password or credit card details.)

Check Links in Emails and on Web Pages

A favourite trick that scammers use is to send an email that looks like it is from a legitimate source – for example, a bank, PayPal, an energy company, a Telco, Apple, your email provider and others.

These emails often include a link that will take to you a page on Safari.

At first glance, the link may appear legitimate – and the page may look like the real thing.

However, the scammers have used very a simple coding trick to hide the real destination of the link while displaying the genuine looking website address.

Staying Safe Online

The link will actually open a fake website that looks just like the website for the company they are pretending to be – and will often ask you to sign in with your email address/user ID and password, or perhaps provide some other private information.

If you do this, the scammers will steal your details and probably gain access to your account – and perhaps other accounts, if you have used the same email address and password elsewhere.

Below is an example of a scam Commonwealth bank email, alongside a real email from the real Commonwealth Ban, showing how these scam emails can look very realistic.

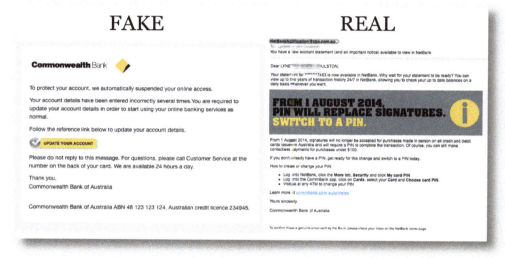

| FAKE | REAL |

It is essential to check the real destination of any links in messages before tapping the link - using a trick we described earlier in this guide.

Just hold your finger on the link to see the underlying web address above the list of options.

Remember that banks, Paypal, eBay, Facebook, etc. will NEVER provide you with a link, and then ask you to confirm or provide your login/password details

The safest approach is to never trust a link you receive in an email, especially one that asks you to confirm account details or other private information. Instead, go directly to the relevant website via your web browser and sign in from there.

Staying Safe Online

If Safari is locked by a nasty message

If you ever receive a nasty message when using Safari – one that seems to 'lock up' your Safari app; or perhaps one that only gives you only one option, and it is an option that you do not want to select (see image on below) – there is no need to panic on an iPad or iPhone.

You have not picked up a virus, spyware or ransomware.

It is quite easy to resolve such a problem - by resetting your Safari browsing history and website data.

Go to **Settings -> Safari** and tap Clear History and Website Data

Once you have done this, you will find that you can start up a fresh Safari session that is free of the fraudster's message.

Other Guides in the Series

Introduction to the iPad and iPhone

iTandCoffee has a wide range of guides about the iPad and iPhone, covering topics like

* **A Guided Tour**

* **The Camera App**

* **The Photos App**

* **Typing and Editing**

* **The Mail App**

* **The Calendar App**

* **The Phone App**

* **Shopping the Stores**

* **Discovering iBooks**

* **Getting Connected**

* And more

Visit www.itandcoffee.com.au/guides for more information.